John Ogilby

The Relation of His Majestie's Entertainment

Passing through the City of London, to His Coronation

John Ogilby

The Relation of His Majestie's Entertainment
Passing through the City of London, to His Coronation

ISBN/EAN: 9783337211790

Printed in Europe, USA, Canada, Australia, Japan

Cover: Foto ©ninafisch / pixelio.de

More available books at **www.hansebooks.com**

CHARLES R.

WHEREAS the Commissioners for the Solemnity of Our Royal Coronation have appointed Our Trusty, and Well-beloved John Ogilby, Gent. for the Conduct of the Poetical part thereof, consisting in Speeches, Emblemes, Mottoes, and Inscriptions, which he intends to set forth in a large Treatise, and Represent in Sculpture; Our will, and pleasure is, That no Person, or Persons whatsoever, do presume to Print, or publish the said Treatise, or any Relation whatsoever, of the said Solemnitie, or Sculpture, in any Size, or Book, or Pamphlet, in any Volume whatsoever, concerning the same, without the Consent of the said John Ogilby, as they will answer the contrary at their peril. Given at our Court at White-hall 11th. day of April in the 13th. Year of our Reign.

By His MAJESTIES Command,

EDVVARD NICHOLAS.

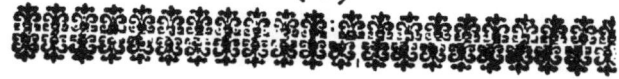

TO THE
RIGHT HONOURABLE
THE
LORD MAYOR,
COURT of ALDERMEN,
COMMON COUNCIL,
COMMITTEE for the
CORONATION,

And the reft of the Worthy Members
of this Honourable *CITY,*

HE RELATION of this Solemnity,
and of what, in purfuit of their Com-
mands, He undertook, and hath Compleated, is Humbly Dedicated by

Their

Most Obedient

Servant,

JOHN OGILBY.

B

HIS

MAJESTIE'S

ENTERTAINMENT

Passing through the City of *LONDON*

TO HIS

CORONATION;

A DESCRIPTION OF THE TRIUMPHAL
ARCHES AND SOLEMNITY.

THE City of *LONDON*, participating the greatest share of that inexpressible Happiness, which these Kingdoms have received by the glorious Restauration of our Soveraign to his Throne, and People, after a tedious Night of Usurpation, and Oppression, and deplorable thraldom in the Late Confusions, have taken the Occasion of His MAJESTIES Coronation to express their Joy with the greatest Magnificence imaginable : imitating therein the antient Romanes, who at the return of their Emperours, erected Arches of Marble, which though They by reason of the shortness of Time could not equal in Materials, yet do theirs far exceed the others in Number, and stupendious Proportions. They have not herein spared any Cost to manifest their affectionate Duty to the *KING*, considering, that, if ever excessive Profusions of this nature might be justified; the present should be allowed, the occasion thereof being the most Miraculous, and Joyful of any, that ever happened. And to the
intent

intent that the ingenuous may be instructed, the Malevolent silenced, and Misinformations prevented, it is thought fit to publish a perfect Description of the Solemnity.

MONDAY, *April* the two and twentieth, His MAJESTY went from the *Tower*, through the City, to *Whitehall*. The Streets were railed all the way on both sides, the Houses, and Windows, adorned with rich Carpets, and Tapistry; on the *North*-side of the Streets; the Companies, with their several *Trophies*, and Ornaments; on the *South*, the Trained Bands.

In his passage through *Chronchild Friers*, He was entertained with Musick. a Band of eight Waits, placed on a Stage.

Near *Algate*, another Band of six Waits received him in like manner with Musick, from a Balcony, built to that Purpose.

In *Leaden-Hall-Street*, near *Lime* Street end, is erected the First Triumphal Arch, after the *Derick Order*. On the *North*-side, on a Pedestal before the Arch, was a Woman personating REBELLION, mounted on a *Hydra*, in a Crimson Robe, torn, Snakes crawling on her habit, and begirt with Serpents, her Hair snaky, a Crown of Fire on her Head, a bloody Sword in one Hand, a charming Rod in the other. Her Attendant CONFUSION, in a deformed Shape, a Garment of several ill-matched Colours; and put on the wrong way; on her Head, Ruins of Castles; torn Crowns, and broken Scepters in each Hand.

On the *South* Pedestal was a representation of BRITTAINS MONARCHY, supported by LOYALTY, both Women: *Monarchy*, in a large Purple Robe, adorn'd with Diadems, and Scepters, over which a Loose Mantle, edg'd with blue and silver Fringe, resembling Water; the Map of *Great Britain* drawn on it, on her Head *London*, in her right Hand, *Edinburgh*; in her left, *Dublin*: *Loyalty* all in White, three Scepters in her right Hand, three Crowns in her left.

The firſt Painting on the *South*-ſide is a Proſpect of His
Majeſtie's Landing at *Dover*-Caſtle, Ships at Sea, great Guns
going off, one kneeling, and kiſſing the King's Hand, Soldi-
ers, Horſe, and Foot, and many People gazing: Above,

ADVENTUS AUG.

The whole Tablet repreſenting His Majeſtie's bleſſed Arrival.
Beneath the Painting this Motto,

IN SOLIDO RURSUS FORTUNA LOCAVIT:

Alluding to that of *Virgil*,

> *Multa dies, variusque labor mutabilis ævi,*
> *Rettulit in melius multos ; alterna reviſens,*
> *Luſit, & in ſolido rurſus Fortuna locavit.*

" The various Work of Time, and many Days,
" Often Affairs from Worſe to Better raiſe;
" Fortune, reviewing thoſe She tumbled down,
" Sporting, reſtores again unto the Crown.

The Painting on the *North*-ſide, oppoſite to this, a Trophy with decollated Heads, having over it,

ULTOR A TERGO DEUS.

Taken out of *Horace*,

> ———*ſequitur Rebelles*
> *Ultor à tergo Deus*———

" God's Vengeance Rebels at the Heels purſues.

This Tablet repreſenting in a Trophy the late Example of
God's Juſtice upon the Rebels, who committed that moſt
horrid Murther upon His Majeſtie's Royal Father of Bleſſed
Memory. To which Rebels the Motto beneath alſo referreth,

AUSI IMMANE NEFAS, AUSÓQUE POTITI:

Said by *Virgil* of thoſe, who were, for the like Crimes, con-
demned

demned to the Pains of *Erebus* ; as he closes the Description
of it in the Sixth of his *Æneis*,

Ausi omnes immane Nefas, ausoque potiti ;

" All dar'd bold Crimes, and thriv'd in what they dar'd.

The Painting over the Middle Arch represents the King,
mounted in Calm Motion, U s u r p a t i o n flying before
him, a Figure with many ill-favoured Heads, some bigger,
some lesser, and one particularly shooting out of his Shoulder,
like C r o m w e l's; Another Head upon his Rump, or
Tayl; two *Harpies* with a Crown chased by an Angel;
Hell's Jaws opening. Under the said Representation of the
King pursuing *Usurpation* is this Motto;

VOLVENDA DIES EN ATTULIT ULTRO.

Taken out of the *Æneis*, lib. 9.

TURNE, *Quod optanti Divum promittere Nemo
Auderet, volvenda dies, en! attulit ultro.*

" What none of all the Gods durst grant implor'd,
" Successive Time yields of its own accord.

Above the *Arch*, on two Pedestals, *South*ward, and *North*-
ward, stand the Statues of King JAMES, and King CHARLS I.
In the Middle, somewat higher, just over the Arch, the Sta-
tue of His Sacred Majesty. Under that of King *James*;

DIVO JACOBO.

Under that of King *Charles* I.

DIVO CAROLO.

Under that of His Majesty this following Inscription;

C   D. N.

D. N.

O

NNIA

MÁ

VENÈ

ER A

O AG

REIP. N

BRIT

OMINU

RITISSIMO

P. P.

Y

I L

RI Q

M RED

OTO

Behind the said Figure, of *Charles* II. in a large Table is de-
ciphered the ROYAL OAK bearing Crowns, and Scepters, instead of Acorns; amongst the Leaves, in a Label,

MIRATURQUE NOVAS FRONDES ET NON SUA POMA.

> ———— " Leaves unknown
> " Admiring, and strange Apples not her Own.

As designing its Reward for the Shelter afforded His Majesty after the Fight at *Worcester* : an expression of *Virgil's*,
speaking of the Advancement of Fruits by the Art of Graffing.

The upper Paintings on the *East*-side are Ruinous, representing the Disorder the Kingdom was in, during His Majestie's Absence; with this Motto,

EN QUO DISCORDIA CIVES!

But on the *West*-side they are finished, to represent the Restauration of our Happiness by His Majestie's Arrival; the
Motto,

FELIX TEMPORUM REPARATIO.

On the *Royal Oak*, in a Label,

ROBUR BRITANNICUM.

Over the Great Table,

REDEUNT SATURNIA REGNA.

Under King *Charles* II.

RESTITUTOR URBIS.

The Painting on the *South-West*-side represents the Lord
Mayor delivering to the King the Keies of the City.

In the *Niches* were four living Figures. The first on the
South-side, a Woman in pleasant Colours; the Emblem on her
Shield, a Terrestrial Globe, the Sun rising, *Bats*, and *Owls* flying
to the Shadow; the Word,

EXCOLCAT CANDOR.

C

The

The Second hath on her Efcutcheon a Swarm of Bees, whetting their stings, the Word,

PRO REGE EXACUUNT.

The Third, on the *North* fide, hath on Her Shield a Mountain burning, Cities, and Vine-yards deftroyed, and ruined; the Word,

IMPIA FOEDERA.

The Fourth hath on Her Efcutcheon an Arm, as it were out of the Clouds; in the Hand a naked Sword: The Motto,

DISCITE JUSTITIAM MONITI.

Eight Mutes above, on Pedeftals; four in White, four in Crimfon.

The Mufick of this Fabrick was ten Drummers, flanking *Rebellion*; twelve Trumpets flanking Monarchy.

Aloft under the two Devaftations, twelve Trumpets, four Drums.

Within the Arch, on two Balconies, fix Trumpets, four Drums.

While the Train paffed along, the Drums beat the Marches of feveral Countries, and the Trumpets founded feveral Levets. At which time, His Majefty drawing near, the Drums' turn their March to a Battel, the Trumpets found a Charge, and on a fudden *Rebellion* rowfeth up her Self, at which, Drums, and Trumpets ceafing, *Rebellion* addreffed to his Majefty the following Speech.

Stand! Stand! who e're you are! this Stage is Ours.
The Names of Princes are infcribed on Flow'rs,
And Wither with them! Stand! You muft Me know,
To Kings, and Monarchy a deadly Fo;
Me, who dare bid You 'midft Your Triumphs Stand,
In the Great City of Your Native Land:

I am

I am Hell's Daughter, Satan's Eldest Childe,
VVhen I first cry'd, the Powers of Darkness smil'd,
And my Glad Father, Thundring at my Birth,
Unhing'd the Poles, and shook the fixed Earth:
My Dear Rebellion (that shall be thy Name,
Said He) Thou Emperours, and Kings shalt tame;
No Right so good, Succession none so long;
But Thou shalt Vanquish by thy Popular Throng,
Those Legions; whicht'enlarge our Pow'r we send
Throughout the V.World, shall Thee (my Dear) attend.
Our mighty Champions, the Sev'n Deadly Sins;
By Malice, Profit, Pleasure, all their Gins,
Bring to Our Kingdom some few spotted Souls;
Thou shalt by Treason hurry them in Shoals.
    VVould You now know what int'rest I have here?
Hidra I ride! great Cities are my Sphear:
I Sorc'ry use, and bag Men in their Beds,
VVith Common-wealths, and Rotas fill their Heads,
Making the Vulgar in Fanetique Swarms——
Court Civil War, and dote on Horrid Arms;
Twas I, who in the late unnatural Broils
Engag'd three Kingdoms, and two Wealthy Isles;
I hope, at last, to march with Flags unfurl'd,
And tread down Monarchie through all the World.

At which Words, Monarchy, and Loyalty, unveiling themselves, Rebellion gave a start as Affrighted; but recollecting
her Self, concluded her Speech thus.

    Ah! Britain, Ah! stand'st thou Triumphant there,
Monarchick Isle? I shake with horrid Fear.
Are thy Wounds whole? Upon thy Cheek fresh Smiles?
Is Joy restor'd to these late mournful Isles?
Ah! must He enter, and a King be Crown'd?
Then, as He riseth, sink we under Ground.

Rebellion having ended her Speech, Monarchy entertained
His Majesty with the following.   D   To

To Hell, foul Fiend, shrink from this glorious Light,
And hide thy Head in Everlasting Night.
Enter in Safety, Royal Sir, this Arch,
And through Your joyful Streets in Triumph march;
Enter, our Sun, our Comfort, and our Life;
No more these Walls shall breed Intestine Strife.
Henceforth Your People onely shall contend
In Loyalty each other to transcend.
May Your Great Actions, and immortal Name,
Be the whole Business, and Delight of Fame.
May You, and Yours, in a Perpetual Calm,
Be Crown'd with Laurel, and Triumphant Palm,
And all Confess, whilst they in you are Blest,
I, MONARCHY, of Governments, am Best.

Monarchy having ended her Speech, the Trumpets sounded
pleasant Levets, and the Drums beat a lofty English March,
whilst His Majesty, the Nobility, & the Rear-Guard passed on.

This Enter-tainment was designed, and the Speeches made by a Person of Quality.

*UPON His Majestie's Advance to the East-India House in
Leaden-Hall-Street, the East-India Company took occasion to
express their dutyful Affections to His Majesty in manner
following.

First, a Youth in Indian Habit, attended by two Black-
Moors, was sent out to bespeak the Kings Expectation,
kneeling before His Horse in these Words;

Stay, Royal Sir, here comes an Indian,
Who brings along a full fraught Caravan
Of perfect Loyalty, and Thanks, to pay,
As Your due Tribute, on this glorious Day.

In the mean while another Youth, in an Indian Vest,
mounted upon a Camel, led out by two Black-Moors, & other
Attendants, the Camel having two Panniers fill'd with
Jewels, Spices, and Silks, to be scattered among the Specta-
tours, addressed himself to His Majesty, as followeth.

Avaunt, you Glorious Trifles of the East,
Pearls, Diamonds, Rubies, Sapphires, and the Best

Of

(11)

Of Aromaticks, and your Silken Toys,
We're Rich enough in our Compleated Joys.
Your Sacred Person, Royal Sir, hath brought
Home all the Wealth, that can be found, or thought
The Riches of both Indies are but Poor,
Compar'd with our renew'd Carolean Store.
We'll blame that Fire no more, that scorch'd our Nest
Of Spicy Trade, since we see You, the Best
Of Kings, Rise from the Ashes of that Flame,
That burnt our First Right Phœnix of Your Name.
For You have out-done Solomon, and made
Provision for a more then Ophir Trade;
Among Your first of unexp-Eled Cares
Enlarg'd our Charter, and dispel'd our Fears
Of the incroaching Holland's Rival Force.
Nor can we doubt, but by the bounteous Source
Of Your Successful Right, not only We,
But all the Merchants of Your Realm shall see
This Empory the Magazine of All
That's Rich, from Phœbus Rising to his Fall;
And Your Imperial Title be the same
In Deed, which Spain's proud Crown wants but inName.
Which Heavens grant! And that we never see
The Sun set on Your Crown, or Dignity.
          Long live King CHARLES the Second.

The two Youths, who speak to His Majesty, as above,
were *John,* and *Samuel Ford,* Sons of Sir *Richard Ford,* one of
the Committees of the *East-India* Company.

The next Entertainment was a Band of six Waits placed
on a Balcony, erected in the Middle of the *North-West* An-
gle of *Leaden-Hall.*

The next Entertainment was at *Corn-hill-*Conduit, on the
top of which stood eight *Nymphs* clad in White, each having
an Escutcheon in one Hand, and a Pendent, or Banner in
the other. On the Tower of the said Conduit, a Noise of
seven Trumpets.

Near

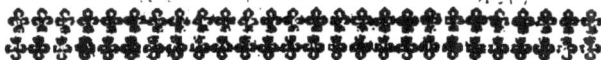

NEAR the *Exchange*, in *Corn-hill*, ſtands the Second *Arch*, which is *Naval*.

On the *Eaſt*-ſide were two Stages erected ; on
each ſide of the Street,one. In that on the *South*-
ſide was a Perſon repreſenting the River *Thames*, his Garment
Looſe and Flowing, Colour Blew and White, waved like
Water, a Mantle over like a Sail ; his Head crown'd with
London-Bridg ; Flags, and Ozier, like long Hair, falling
o're his Shoulders, his Beard long, Sea-green, and White,
curl'd ; an Oar in his right Hand, the Model of a Ship in his
left, an Urn beſide him, out of which iſſues Water ; four Attendants in White, repreſenting the four freſh Streams, which
fall into the River *Thames*, viz. *Charwell*, *Lea*, *Colne*, and
Medway.

In the other Stage, on the *North*-ſide, which is made
like the upper Deck of a Ship, were three *Seamen*, whereof one habited like a *Boat-ſwain*,

A Shield, or Table, in the front of the *Arch*, bears
this *Inſcription*.

NEPTUNO BRITÁNNICO,

CAROLO II,

CUJUS ARBITRIO

MARE

VEL LIBERUM, VEL CLAUSUM.

The

The first Painting, on the *North*-side over the City-Arms, represents NEPTUNE, with his Trident advanced; the *Inscription*,

NEPTUNO REDUCI

On the *South*-side, opposite, MARS, with his Spear inverted, his Shield charged with a *Gorgon*; by his Knees the Motto,

MARTI PACIFERO.

Over the *Arch*, the Marriage of *Thame*, and *Isis*.

The Painting on the *North*-side, over *Neptune*, represents the EXCHANGE; the Motto,

——GENERIS LAPSI SARCIRE RUINAS.

An Expression of *Virgil's*, *Georg.* 4. speaking of the Industry of *Bees*, never discouraged by their Losses; his Description of it running thus,

Quò magis exhausta fuerint, hoc acrius omnes
Incumbent generis lapsi sarcire Ruinas,
Complebuntque Foros, & Floribus Horrea texent.

How much by Fortune they exhausted are,
So much they strive the Ruins to repair
Of their fal'n Nation, and they fill th'Exchange,
Adorning with the choicest Flow'rs their Grange.

The Painting on the *South*-side, over *Mars*, shews the Tower of *London*; the *Inscription*,

CLAUDUNTUR BELLI PORTÆ.

The Pedestals, in the Upper Story, are Adorned with eight living Figures, representing EUROPE, ASIA, AFRICK, and AMERICA, with Escutcheons, and Pendents, bearing the Arms of the Companies, Trading into those Parts.

The uppermost great *Table* in the fore-ground repre-
E   sents

sent. King *Charles the First*, with the Prince, now *Charles* the *Second*, in His Hand, viewing the *Soveraign of the* Sea, the Prince leaning on a Cannon; the *Inscription*, as

O NIMIUM DILECTE DEO, CUI MILITAT
    ÆQUOR,
ET CONJURATI VENIUNT AD CLASSICA
    VENTI.

For thee, O Jove's Delight, the Seas engage,
And Muster'd Winds, draw up in Battel, Rage.

Above, over the *Cornich*, between the two Celestial *Hemi-sphres*, an *Atlas*, bearing a *Terrestrial Globe*, and on it a Ship under Sail; the Word,

UNUS NON SUFFICIT.

The great Painting on the *West*-side represents the Duke of YORK, habited *à l'antique*, like *Neptune*, standing on a Shell drawn by *Sea-Horses*, in one Hand a *Trident*, the Reins in the other; his Motto,

SPES ALTERA.

On the four *Niches* within the *Arch* were living Figures, with Escutcheons, and Pendents, representing ARITHME-TICK, GEOMETRY, ASTRONOMY, and NAVIGA-TION.

Arithmetick, a Woman habited *à l'antique*, upon her Vestment Lines, with *Musick*-Notes on them : In her Escut-cheon a Book opened, with a Hand, pointing to the Figures 1. 2. 3. 4, &c. under,

PAR ET IMPAR.

Geometry, a Woman in a pleasant *Green*, in her Shield a *Compass*, and a *Triangle*; the Inscription,

DESCRIPSIT RADIO TOTUM QUÆ GEN-
    TIBUS ORBEM.

                                        Astronomy

Astronomy, a Woman in a loose Vestment, *Azure*, wrought with Stars of Gold, looking up to Heaven; in her Shield a Table, wherein are diverse *Astronomical Figures*; the *Inscription*,

CIRCUMSPICIT ORIONA.

Taken out of the third of the *Æneis*, where the *Poet* Introduces *Palinurus*, contemplating the Heavens.

Navigation, a Woman in Sea-green Habit, in her Escutcheon an *Anchor*, with a *Cable* about it; the *Inscription*,

TUTUM TE LITTORE SISTAM.

While the *Nobility* passed the *Triumphal Arch*, the three Sea-men Entertained them with this Song from the Stage on the *North-side* of the *Arch*,

From Neptune's VVatry Kingdomes, where
Storms, and Tempests rise so often,
As would the VVorld in Pieces tear,
Should Providence their Rage not soften,
In that fluctuating Sphere,
VVhere stout Ships, and smaller Barks
Are toss'd like Balls, or feather'd Corks,
VVhen Briny VVaves to Mountains swell,
VVhich dimming oft Heav'ns glittring Sparks,
    Then descending low as Hell;
        Through this Crowd,
        In a Cloud,
By a strange and unknown Spell,
    VVe newly Landing,
    Got this Standing,
All Merry Boys, and Loyal,
    Our Pockets full of Pay
    This Triumphal Day,

To

To make of our skill a Tryal,
   Of our little little skill :
   Let none then take it ill,
We must have no Denyal.

II.

We, who have rais'd, and laid the Poles,
   Plough'd Frozen Seas, and scalding Billows,
Now stiff with Cold, then scorch'd on Coals,
   Ships our Cradles, Decks our Pillows ;
'Mongst threatning Rocks, and treach'rous Shoals,
   Through Gibraltar's contracted Mouth,
And Realms condemn'd to Heat and Drowth,
   Or Baltick Waves bound up in Ice,
Or Magellan as Cold, though South,
   Our good Fortune, in a trice,
     Through this Crowd,
     In a Cloud,
Brings us where, in Paradise,
    We newly Landing,
    Got this Standing,
All Merry Boys, and Loyal,
    Our Pockets full of Pay
    This Triumphal Day,
To make of our skill a Tryal,
   Of our little little skill :
   Let none then take it ill,
We must have no Denyal.

III.

VVe, who so often bang'd the Turk,
   Our Broad-sides speaking Thunder,
Made Belgium striks, and proud Dunkirk,
   VVho liv'd by Prize, and Plunder,
And routed the Sebastian Shirk ;

We paid their Poops, and painted Beaks,
Cleans'd before and eft their Decks,
Till their Scuppers ran with Gore,
VVhil'ft in as faft falt-VVater breaks ;
But we are Friends of this no more :
Through this Crowd
In a Cloud,
VVe have found an happy Shore,
And newly Landing,
Got this Standing ;
All Merry Boys, and Loyal,
Our Pockets full of Pay
This Triumphal Day,
To make of our skill a Trial
Of our little little skill,
Let none then take it ill,
We muft have no denyal.

Befides the three beforenamed, who fung the precedent
Song, there were in like manner habited, like Sea-men, fix
other Perfons, who made a Wind-Mufick.

The Mufick in the Stage confifted of three Drums, and fix
Trumpets.

On the *Eaft*-fide, Winde-Mufick, confifting of fix Perfons.

On two Balconies, within the *Arch*, Winde-Mufick
confifting of twelve Perfons.

On the *Weft*-Gallery were placed fix Trumpets.

Thefe, and all the other Mufick, belonging to this Triumph, performed their Duty without Intermiffion, till fuch
time as His Majefty fronted the *Figure*, which reprefented
Thames, and then ceafed ; upon which *Thames* made the
enfuing *Speech*.

F   Ten

TEn Moons, Great Sir, their silver Crescents fill'd,
  Since, mounted on a Billow, I beheld
  You on the Bridg; but louder Joys there were,
That barr'd my Welcomes from Your Sacred Ear:
Now I above my highest Bound have rear'd
My Head, to say what could not, then, be heard.

  Hail, Mighty Monarch! whose Imperial Hand
Quiets the Ocean, and secures the Land;
This City, whom I serve with Neighb'ring Floods,
Exporting Yours, importing Foreign Goods,
With anxious Grief, did long Your Absence mourn;
Now with full Joy she Welcomes Your Return;
Your blest Return! by which she is restor'd
To all the Wealth Remotest Lands afford.
At your Approach, I hasten'd to the Downs,
To see Your Moving Forts, Your Floating Towns;
Your Sovereigns, Big with Thunder, Plow the Main,
And swimming Armies in their Womb contain.
You are our Neptune, every Port, and Bay
Your Chambers, the whole Sea is Your High-way.
Though sev'ral Nations Boast their Strength on Land,
Yet You Alone the wat'ry World command.

  Pardon, great Sir, fair Cynthia checks my stay;
But to Your Royal Palace, twice a day,
I will repair; there my proud Waves shall wait,
To bear our Cæsar, and His conqu'ring Fate.

  The River *Thames* having ended his Speech, the three
Seamen, who entertain'd the Nobility with the former
Song, addressed the following to His Majesty.

King

I.

King CHARLS, King CHARLS, great Neptune of the Main!
Thy Royal Navy rig,
And We'll not care a fig
For France, for France, the Netherlands, nor Spain;
The Turk, who looks so big,
We'll whip him like a Gig
About the Mediterrane,
His Gallies all sunk, or ta'ne.
We'll seize on their Goods, and their Monies,
Those Algier Sharks,
That Plunder Ships, and Barks,
Algier, Sally, and Tunis,
VVe'll give them such Toasts
On the Barbary-Coasts,
Shall drive them to their Harbours, like Conies.
Tantara rantantan
Tantara ran tan tara,
Nor all the world we fear-a;
The great Fish-pond
Shall be thine-a
Both here and beyond,
From Strand to Strand,
And underneath the Line-a.

II.

A Sail, a Sail, I to the Offin see,
She seems a lusty Ship;
Hoise all your Sails a-trip:
VVe'll weather, weather her, what e're she be:
Your Helm then steady keep,
And Thunder up the Deep,
A Man of VVar no Merchant She;
VVe'll set her on her Crupper;
Give Fire, Bounce, Bounce,
Pickeering Villains trounce,

Till

Till Blood run in Streams at the Scupper ;
Such a Break-fast them we shall
Give with Powder, and Ball,
They shall need neither Dinner, nor Supper.
Tan tara ran tan tan
Tan tara ran tan tara,
Pickeering Rogues ne're spare-a ;
VVith Bullets pink
Their Quarters ;
Untill they stink,
They sink, they sink,
Farewell the Devil's Martyrs.

III.

They yield, they yield ; shall we the poor Rogues spare ?
Their ill-gotten Goods,
Preserv'd from the Floods,
That King CHARLES, and we may share ?
VVith Wine then chear our Bloods,
And putting off our Hoods,
Drink to His MAJESTIE bare,
The King of all Compassion :
On our Knees next fall
T'our Royal Admiral,
A Health for his Preservation,
Dear JAMES the Duke of YORK,
Till our Heels grow light as Cork,
The second Glory of our Nation.
Tan tara ran tan tan
Tan tara ran tan tara,
To the Royal Pair-a,
Let every man
Full of Wine
Take off his Can,
Though wan though wan,
To make his red Nose shine-a.

The

(21)

The Seamen having ended their Song, the several sorts of
Musick performed their Duty, whilst His Majesty passed on
towards *Cheap-side.*

At the *Stocks,* the Entertainment was a Body of Military
Musick, placed on a Balcony, consisting of six Trumpets,
and three Drums. the Fountain there being after the *Thuscan*
Order, venting Wine, and Water.

In like manner, on the Top of the great *Conduit,* at the Entrance of *Cheap-side,* was another Fountain, out of which
issued both Wine, and Water, as in a Representation of
Temperance ; and on the several Towers of that Conduit were
eight Figures, habited like *Nymphs,* with Escutcheons in one
Hand, and Pendents or Banners in the other : And between
each of them, Wind-Musick ; the number, eight.

On the Standard also in *Cheap-side* there was a Band of Waits
placed, consisting of six Persons.

At some Distance from the Standard were seated the *Aldermen* in Scarlet, in Seats covered, where His Majesty being
come, was entertained with the ensuing *Speech,* by Sir *William
Wild,* Knight and Baronnet, the *Recorder* of the City.

Most Gracious Sovereign,

TO *declare the Happiness of Your People in the Enjoyment of
this glorious Day, is a Subject for an* Angel *not a* Man.
It is not long since, Most Mighty Prince (*But yet 'twas long, Sir,*)
*that, for want of Your Royal Presence, Your People were miserably en-
tangled in, and infested with, many Sad and destructive Revolutions;
such, that thereby so violent a Sea of Confusion, and Disorder, was
broke in upon them that their Lives, Liberties, Estates, and that,
which is most dear to all Good Men, their very Religion (the best Re-
form'd throughout the* World) *were ready to have been swallow-
ed up.*

*But no sooner did Your Glorious Person appear amongst them,
but those furious Waters did abate, and that Black Cloud of Misery,
and Calamity, from thence exhaled, and ready to fall upon them,*

G   was

was dispers'd and gone, and they, in a full Carrere to their Pristine
Glory, and Happiness.

And now by this time, Most Puissant King, I make no Question,
but all Your People, I am sure Your Loyal Ones, and I have Charity
enough, to hope they will all prove such, are fully satisfi'd, that because
it was in England, as sometimes twas in Israel, that they had no
King amongst them, therefore their latter days were so Calamitous;
Quod tot tantaque mala conciliarat non habuisse Regem.

But to the Everlasting Praise of our good God, we have now, not
only a King amongst us, but such a King, which is a Blessing to
His People, not of a Mushroom Descent, but the Son of Nobles, of a
most Royal Stem, not intituled to his Kingdoms by Perjury, and Vil-
lany, but by an Ancient and Undoubted Right, A KING, of whom
it may be truly said that, had all that Clemency, Goodness, and
Sweetness of Temper proper to a Prince, and advantageous to a
People, been totally lost, they are all reunited, and concentred in His
Royal Person.

And therefore, as I said at first, of our Happiness, give me leave,
Most Illustrious Prince, to say also of our Joys, their Declarati-
on is an Angelical Employment, Matter in truth, rather of Admiration, then for Expression. *Exigua gaudia loquuntur, ingentia
stupent:* Onely let me say this, and I hope I may say it with a Pious
Allusion,

This is the Day, which the Lord hath made, we will
Rejoyce, and be Glad in it.

And that our Joys may not be short-liv'd, Your Happiness, and
Our Joys being like Hippocrates his Twins, must live and Dy
together.

May Your Days be many, Your Reign ever peaceful, and prosper-
ous, and Your Posterity Numerous; May Your Feet be always upon
the Neck of Your Enemies; Let them be ever Blessed, which shall
Bless You; and Cursed be they, which shall Curse You; and let all
Your People say, Amen.

I know well, Most Mighty King, that neither the Time, nor
the Place, will admit of any long Discourse; and that I now speak not
only to Solon, but a Solomon; One, that is no Friend to many
words, as well knowing, in multiloquio non deest Peccatum;

And

And therefore be pleas'd to give Your Servant leave in a Word to deliver his Errand, which is in the Name of this Ancient and renowned City, most Cordially to congratulate Your Gracious Accession hither this Day, upon this solemn, and glorious Occasion, and as a pure signal of that true Allegiance, and Duty, which they owe to Your Sacred Majesty, humbly to present unto Your Royal Hands this Purse of Gold; which let me assure You, comes from free Hearts, full of Loyalty, and Fidelity, the Best of Presents to a Gracious King; and therefore I am confident, that as they offer it chearfully, Your Majesty will vouchsafe to accept it Graciously. I have done Sir, and have no more to say, but this,

God Save the K i n g.

The *Speech* ended, Sir *William*, in the Name of the City, made an Humble Present to His Majesty of a Purse of Gold, in Testimony of their Dutifull Affection.

The

T HE third Triumphal *Arch* ſtands near *Wood*-ſtreet end, not far from the Place, where the *Croſs* ſometimes ſtood. It repreſents an Artificial Building of two Stories, one after the *Corinthian* way of Architecture, the other after the *Compoſite*, repreſenting the *Temple* of *Concord*; with this Inſcription on a Shield,

ÆDEM

CONCORDIÆ
IN HONOREM OPTIMI PRINCIPIS,
CUJUS ADVENTU
BRITANNIA TERRA MARIQ. PACATA,
ET PRISCIS LEGIBUS REFORMATA EST,
AMPLIOREM SPLENDIDIORIMQ.
RESTITUIT,
S. P. Q. L.

In

In the Spandrils of the *Arch* were two Figures, in Female Habits, leaning : One representing P E A C E, the other T R U T H. That of *Peace* had her Shield charged with an *Helmet*, and Bees issuing forth, and going into it ; the Word,

PAX BELLO POTIOR.

Truth on the other side, in a thin Habit, on her Shield T I M E, bringing *Truth* out of a Cave ; the Word,

TANDEM EMERSIT.

Over the great Painting upon the *Arch* of the *Cupula*, represents a large G E R Y O N with three Heads, crowned, in his three right-Hands a *Lance*, a *Sword*, and a *Scepter*; in his three left-Hands the three Escutcheons of *England Scotland* and *Ireland*; before him the King's Arms with three Imperial Crowns; beneath, in great Letters,

CONCORDIA INSUPERABILIS.

On the top of the *Cupula*, C O N C O R D, a Woman, in her right-Hand holding her Mantle, in her left-Hands Discord as under her Feet, a Serpent struggling, which she seems to tread down.

On the West-side, the third great Figure, a Woman, standing at the Prow of a Ship; in her left hand, a *Cornucopia*; the Word,

FORTUNÆ REDUCI.

Above were eight living Figures with Pennons, and Shields, representing the four *Cardinal* Virtues, each with an Attendant.

P R U D E N C E, on her Shield *Bellerophon* on a *Pegasus*, runing his Javelin into the Mouth of a *Chymera*; the word,

CONSILIO ET VIRTUTE.

H   JUSTICE

JUSTICE, on her Shield a Woman holding a Sword in one
Hand, a Balance in the other ; the Word,

QUOD DEXTERA LIBRAT.

TEMPERANCE, a Viol in her left Hand, a Bridle in her
right; the Word,

FERRE LUPATA DOCET.

FORTITUDE, a Lyon having the Arms of *England*, in
an Escutcheon ; the Word,

CUSTOS FIDISSIMUS.

The internal part of this Triumph, or Temple, is round,
the upper part Dark, onely enlightned by Artificial Lights ;
the lower part divided into ten Parts by Pilasters, with Pedestals.

Within the Table are twelve living Figures, three
placed above the Rest.

The First the *Goddess* of the Temple in rich Habit, with
a *Caduceus* in her Hand, and a *Serpent* at her Feet. Behind
the *Goddess*, a Man in a Purple Gown, like a Citizen of London, presenting the KING with an *Oaken* Garland. Over the
KING's Head,

PATER PATRIÆ.

Over the Citizen's,

S. P. Q. L.

OB CIVES SERVATOS.

The Second, *Truth*, standing next the *Goddess* CONCORD,
in a thin, but rich Habit, her Shield charg'd with a Book
held open, with wings fastn'd by a Chain to a Cloud ; beneath, a *Fury* plucking at the end of the Chain ; the word,

VERITAS INVICTA.

The

The Third, LOVE richly dress'd, on the other side of the *Goddess*; on her Shield a *Cupid*, Roses in his right hand, in his left a Fish.

Of the nine Figures; the first bears, on a Shield, the King of *Bees* flying alone; a Swarm following at some distance; the word,

REGE INCOLUMI MENS OMNIBUS UNA.

The Second, on his Shield, a *Testudo* advancing against a Wall; the Word,

CONCORDIÆ CEDUNT.

The Third, a Shield charged with Hearts; the Word,

HIC MURUS AHENEUS ESTO.

The Fourth, like a spread-Eagle with two Heads, one of an *Eagle*, the other of an *Estrich*; in the Mouth of the *E-strich* an Horse-shoe, in the Talons of the Eagle a Thunderbolt; the Word,

PRÆSIDIA MAJESTATIS.

The Fifth, a Bundle of Javelins; the Word,

UNITAS.

The Sixth, two Hands joyned athwart the Escutcheon, as from the Clouds, holding a *Caduceus* with a Crown; the Word,

FIDE ET CONSILIO.

The Seventh, Arms laid down, Guns, Pikes, Ensigns, Swords; the Word,

CONDUNTUR NON CONTUNDUNTUR.

The Eight, a *Caduceus*, with a winged Hat above, and Wings beneath, two Cornucopiæ coming out at the middle, supported by a Garland; the Word,

VIRTUTI FORTUNA COMES.

Th

The Ninth, a Bright *Star* striking a gleam through the midst of the Efcutcheon; the Word,

MONSTRANT REGIBUS ASTRA VIAM.

With thefe Figures was intermingled a Band of twenty four Violins.

The Bafes, and Capitals within this *Triumph*, are as Brafs, and the Pillars Steel.

The Triumph thus adorned, and the feveral Mufick playing, all paffed through, till fuch time as His Majefty came to the middle of the Temple, at which time the three principal living Figures, viz. CONCORD, LOVE, and TRUTH, who till then had not been feen, were, by the drawing of a Curtain difcovered, and entertained His Majefty with the following Song.

I.

Comes not here the King of Peace,
Who the Stars fo long foretold,
From all Wars fhould us releafe
Converting Iron-times to Gold?

II.

Behold, Behold!
Our Prince confirm'd by Heav'nly figns
Brings healing Balm,
Brings healing Balm, and Anodines,
To clofe our Wounds, and Pain affwage.

III.

He comes with conquering Bays, and Palm,
Where fwelling Billows us'd to rage,
Gliding on a filver Calm;
Proud Interefts now no more engage,

Chorus.

Let thefe Arched Roofs refound,
Joyning Inftruments, and Voice,

Fright

Fright pale Spirits under Ground;
   But let Heav'n and Earth rejoyce,
We our Happiness have found.
He, thus marching to be Crown'd,
   Attended with this glorious Train,
     From civil Broils
     Shall free these, Isles,
VVhilst Hee and his Posterity shall reign.

I.

VVho follow Trade or Study Arts,
   Improving Pasture, or the Plow,
Or furrow Vraves to foreign Parts,
   Use Your whole Endeavours now.

II

      His Brow, his Brow
Bids you Hearts, as well as Hands,
      Together joyn,
  Together joyning bless these Lands;
Peace, and Concord, never poor.

III.

VVill make with VVealth these Streets to shine,
   Ships freight with Spice, and Golden Ore,
Your Fields with Honey, Milk, and VVine,
   To supply our Neighbours Store.

   The First Song ended, Concord addressed her self to His Majesty, in these Words,

   Welcome, great Sir, to CONCORD's Fane,
   VVhich Your Return built up again;

I   You

You have her Fabrick rear'd so high;
That the proud Turrets kiss the Skie.
Tumult by You, and Civil War
In Janus Gates imprison'd are ;
By You the King of Truth, and Peace,
May all Divisions ever cease !
Your Sacred Brow the Blushing Rose,
And Virgin Lilly twin'd inclose !
The Calcedonian Thistle-Down
Combine with these t'adorn Your Crown !
No Discord in th' Hibernian Harp !
Nought in our Duty flat, or sharp !
But all conspire that You, as Best,
May 'bove all other Kings be blest.

The Speech ended, His Majesty, at His going off, was
entertained with the following Song.

With all our Wishes, Sir, go on,
   Our Charles, three Nations Glory ;
That Worlds of Eys may look upon,
   Behinde, Sir, and before Ye ;
Go great Exemplar of our British Story,
      Paternal Crowns assume,
      That then Your Royal Name
      May, registred by Fame,
      Smell like a sweet Perfume :
Not writ in Marble, Brass, or Gold,
      Nor sparkling Gems,
      Such as shine in Diadems,
   But where all Nations may behold
      With brighter Characters enroll'd,
On th' Azure Vellum of Configur'd Stars ;
      Who fixt with gentle Smiles
      Two floating Isles,
And built well-grounded Peace on Civil Wars.

On

On the little Conduit, at the lower End of *Cheap-fide*, were placed four Figures, or *Nymphs*, each of them having an Efcutcheon in the one Hand, and a Pendent in the other.

In a Balcony, erected at the Entrance of *Pater-nofter*-Row, were placed His Majeftie's Drums, and Fife; the number of Perfons, eight.

In St. *Paul's-Church*-Yard, upon a Scaffold, erected to that purpofe, ftood the children of *Chrifts*-Hofpital in blew-Coats, upon His Majeftie's approach, one of them entertained him with the following Speech.

--- - - - - - - -

Dread Sovereign,

HIftory, tells us, that fuch piercing Raies darted forth from King *Philip's* countenance, as dazled the eyes of *Demofthenes* the Oratour fo much, that his voluble Tongue forgate its duty, and was lock'd up in filence.

Much more might I fear the like to befal me, being now before fo glorious a Sun, as may well dazle the Eyes of fo poor a Nothing as I am. Who am I, that I fhould adventure to invite the Ears of fo great a Majefty to fo contemptible a found, and the Eyes of fuch a Glory to the beholding my felf, and thefe vile Abjects ? But I have heard, that as there is a Majeftick Glory in Your Perfon, fo there is a Royal Goodnefs in Your Difpofition. This hath emboldned this poor Duft to befeech You to accept of two Mites from thefe the loweft, and meaneft of all Your Subjects.

Our firft Mite is the expreffion of our Joy for Your Majeftie's wonderful prefervation in Your abfence, Your fafe arrival to us, and Your prefence among us. This Year may well be called *The Year of Wonders* ; and this Day of Your Solemnity may be termed *The Birth-day of England's Happinefs*, and therefore deferves to be regiftred in the Kalendar of the Hearts of all Loyal Subjects.

We

We have all seen those *Magnalia Dei* plainly discovered, and have observed the Wheels of Divine Providence in a seeming contrariety; yet the motion at last to be true and regular. Blessed be that God, that in the midst of all our dismal Conflagrations did provide your Majesty a *Zoar* to rest in, and now at last hath so calm'd those Storms, and State-convulsions, that You may this day encircle your Royal Brows with a glorious Crown, and be advanced to your Throne in much Serenity.

But Mites, as they are of no great value, so they are pieces of no great quantity: I shall therefore offer up our second, which is a *Mite of Prayer*, and then cease to put farther stop to this daies Solemnity.

We have two Petitions, the one *to*, the other *for* your Majesty. We humbly beseech you (Most Dread Sovereign) that as at first EDWARD the Sixth, who once sway'd the Scepter of this Kingdom, laied a foundation for the Reception of poor Orphans, who have since been upheld by all Your Royal Ancestours, especially your late Father of blessed Memory; so You would shine upon us still by Your Gracious favour, and Princely indulgence. There are above Eleven hundred of us, part whereof have in the Name of all, presented themselves this day as lively Monuments of God's mercy, and real Objects of Christian charity : for whom through the pious care, and faithful industry of the Right Honourable the Lord *Mayor*, *Aldermen*, *Governours*, and liberal *Benefactours*, a Table hath been spread, and other Necessaries both for Soul, and Body afforded, even in the midst of those Exigencies, that exposed others to Want, and Penury.

But I am afraid any longer (Most Gracious Sovereign) to detain Your Royal Ears, with childish Smatterings. I have done.

Heaven grant You long to live, and prosperously to Reign over us, that when You have finished God's work, having
saic

sate upon this Earthly Throne Beloved, You may leave it Lamented.

In the mean time, let Orphans eccho forth with graceful acclamations,

God bless King CHARLES *the Second.*

Between that and *Ludgate*, there were two other Balconies erected: In one was placed a Band of six Waits; In the other, six Drums.

On the Top of *Ludgate* six Trumpets.

At *Fleet*-Bridge a Band of six Waits.

On *Fleet*-Conduit were six Figures, or *Nymphs* clad in White, each with an Escutcheon in one Hand, and a Pendent in the other, as also a Band of six Waits. And on the *Lanthorn* of the Conduit was the Figure of *Temperance*, mixing Water and Wine.

K   IN

***

IN *Fleetſtreet*, near *White-Friers*, ſtands the Fourth Triumphal Arch, repreſenting the *Garden* of PLENTY; it is of two Stories, one of the *Dorick* Order, the other of the *Ionick*. The Capitals have not their juſt Meaſure, but incline to the Modern *Architecture*.

Upon the great Shield, over the *Arch*, in large Capitals, this Inſcription,

UBERITATI

AUG.

EXTINCTO BELLI CIVILIS INCENDIO

CLUSOQ. JANI TEMPLO

ARAM CELSISS.

CONSTRUXIT.

S. P. Q. L.

Over

Over the *Postern*, on the *South*-side of the Entrance is
BACCHUS, in a Chariot, drawn by *Leopards*, his Mantle
a *Panther's* Skin; his Crown, of *Grapes*, a *Thyrsus* with
Ivy in his left Hand; a *Cup* in his right: underneath,

LIBER PATER.

The Painting over this represents SILENUS on his Ass,
Satyres dancing round about, in Drunken, and Antick Po-
stures; the Prospect, a *Vine ya d.*

On the *North*-side opposite, *Ceres*, drawn in a Chariot by
winged *Dragons*, and crowned with Ears of Corn, in her
left Hand, Poppy; in her right, a blazing Torch. The
Painting over her is a Description of *Harvest*; with

CERES AUG.

On the *West* side of the Arch, over the *South Postern*, the
Goddess FLORA, in a various Coloured Habit; in one Hand,
Red and white *Roses*; in the other, *Lillies*; on her Head, a
Garland of several other Flowers.
The Painting over this, a Garden, with Walks, Statues,
Fountains, Flowers, and Figures of Men and Women walk-
ing.
Opposite to this, on the *North*-side, the *Goddess* POMONA,
crown'd with a Garland of several Fruits; in her right Hand,
the Sun; in her left Hand, a Wand; At her Feet all sorts of
Graffing, and Gardening Tools.
The Painting above, an *Orchard.*
On the Corners four living Figures; above, the four Sea-
sons of the Year.
In the *Niches* stood four Figures, representing the four
Winds.

EURUS

Eurus, a *Black-Moor* with Black wings! his Embleme, the Sun rising, and a fair plain Country ; his Motto,

AD AURORAM NABATHÆAQ. REGNA.

Boreas, instead of Feet, two Serpents Tails, his Wings covered with Snow ; his Emblem, a Rocky Mountainous Country, and the *Pleiades* rising over it ; his Motto,

SCYTHIAM SEPTEMQ. TRIONES
HORRIFER INVADIT——

Auster, in a dark-coloured Habit, with Wings like Clouds, his Emblem, a Cloudy Sky, and Showres, his Motto,

NUBIBUS ASSIDUIS PLUVIAQ. MADESCIT.

Zephyrus, like an *Adonis* with Wings ; the Emblem a Flowery Plain ; the Word,

——TEPENTIBUS AURIS
DEMULCET——

The great Figure on the top of all represented PLENTY, crowned, a Branch of Palm in her right Hand, a *Cornucopiæ* in her left.

The Musick aloft on both sides, and on the two Balconies within, were twelve Waits, six Trumpets, and three Drums.

At a convenient distance before this structure, were two Stages erected, divided, planted, and adorned like Gardens, each of them eight Yards in length, five in breadth. Upon that on the *North*-side sate a Woman representing PLENTY, crowned with a Garland of diverse Flowers, clad in a green Vestment embroidered with Gold, holding a *Cornucopiæ* : Her Attendants, two Virgins.

At His Majeſtie's approach to the *Arch*, this Perſon, repreſenting P L E N T Y riſing up, made addreſs to Him in theſe
Words;

> *Great Sir ; the Star, which at Your Happy Birth*
> *Joy'd with his Beams (at Noon) the wondring Earth,*
> *Did with auſpicious Luſtre, then, preſage*
> *The Glitt'ring Plenty of this Golden Age ;*
> *The Cloud's blown o're, which long our joys o'recaſt,*
> *And, the ſad Winter of Your abſence paſt,*
> *See ! the three ſmiling Seaſons of the Year*
> *Agree at once to bid You Welcome here,*
> *Her Homage Dutious Flora comes to pay ;*
> *With Her Enamel'd Treaſure ſtrows Your Way :*
> *Ceres, and Pales with a bounteous Hand,*
> *Diffuſe their Plenty over all Your Land ;*
> *And Bacchus is ſo Laviſh of his Store,*
> *That Wine flows now where Water ran before.*
> *Thus Seaſons, Men, and Gods their Joys expreſs,*
> *To ſee Your Triumph, and our Happineſs.*

His Majeſty, having paſſed the four Triumphal *Arches*, was
at *Temple-Bar* entertained with the View of a Delightfull Bo-
ſcage, full of ſeveral Beaſts, both Tame, and Savage, as alſo
ſeveral living Figures, and Muſick of eight Waits. But this,
being the Limit of the Citie's Liberty, muſt be ſo likewiſe
of our Deſcription.

L   THE

THE *Common-Council* of *London* appointed a Committee for the managing these Entertainments of His Sacred M A J E S T Y, which confifted of nine *Aldermen*, and fifteen *Commoners*, and others: their Names, thefe;

Aldermen,

Sir *Tho. Adams*, Knight *and* Baronet.
Mr. *Ald. Fowk*.
Sir *Tho. Aleyn*, Knight *and* Baronet.
Sir *VVilliam Thompfon*, Knight.
Sir *Jo. Frederick*, Knight.
Sir *Jo. Robinfon*, Knight *and* Baronet.
Sir *Antho. Bateman*, Knight.
Sir *Jo. Lawrence* Knight.
Sir *Richard Ford*, Knight.

Commoners,

Sir *Will. Bateman*, Knight.
Sir *Lau. Bromfield*, Knight.
Sir *Tho. Bludworth*, Knight.
Sir *Jo. Cutler*, Knight *and* Baronet.
Sir *Theoph. Bidulph*, Knight.
Sir *Will. Vincent* Knight.
Deputy *Aylmer*.
Deputy *Hickman*.
Mr. *Saunders*.
Colonel *Truffel*.
Colonel *Clagett*.
Mr. *Penning*,
Colonel *Nevil*.
Mr. *Ofbaldfton*.
Mr. *Mafcal*.

Thefe Worthy Members of this Honourable *City*, in Order to this *Solemnity*, raifed Confiderable Sums of Money, which by the feveral Companies were freely Contributed, in expreffion of their Loyalty,

THE

THE *Parts, of which this* Entertainment *consists, were carried on by several Persons, who performed all to* Admiration, *and, considering the Shortness of the Warning, much beyond what could have been imagined.*

The Architectural Part *by* Mr. Peter Mills, *Surveyour of the* City, *and another Person, who desires to have his Name conceal'd.*

The Carpentry, *by* Mr. John Scot, *Mr* William Pope, Mr. Thomas Wratton, *and Mr.* Roger Jerman.

The Painting, *by Mr.* William Lightfoot, *and Mr.* Andrew Dacres.

The Joyner's Work, *by Mr.* Thomas Whiting.

The Carvers VVork, *by Mr.* Richard Cleer.

The Principal *Parts of the* Musick, *by His* Majestie's *Servants :* All Composed *by* Matthew Lock, *Esq;* Composer *in Ordinary to His* Majesty.

THE

THE

CAVALCADE,

OR

His *MAJESTIES* paſſing through the *CITY* of

LONDON

TOWARDS HIS

CORONATION,

Monday, April 22.

The Duke of York's Horſe-guard.
Meſſengers of the Chambers, in their Coats with the
Kings Arms before and behind.

Cloaks {
Eſquires to the Knights of the Bath, in number 40.
Knight Harbinger } { Serjeant Porter.
Sewers of the Chamber.
Gent. Uſhers, Quarter-Waiters *in number*   8.

Gowns {
Clerks of the Chancery   ſix.
Clerks of the Signet   four.
Clerks of the Privy-Seal.

Cloaks { Clerks of the Council   four.

Gowns {
Clerks of the Parliament   } two.
Clerks of the Crown   two.

Gowns, and
Squart Caps } Chaplains having Dignities, *ten in number*.

Gowns {
The King's Advocate } { The King's Remembrancer.
Maſters of the Chancery.
The King's learned Council at Law.   two.

Gowns {
The Kings puiſne Serjeants   two.
The King's Attorney } { The King's Sollicitour.
The Kings Eldeſt Serjeants   two.

M

Gowns

Gowns {	Two Secretaries of the *French*, and *Latine* Tongue.	
Cloaks {	Gentlemen-Ushers, daily-Waiters.	
Cloaks {	Sewers Carvers } in Ordinary. Cup-bearers	
Cloaks {	Esquiers of the Body	four.
	Masters of standing Offices, viz.	
Cloaks {	Tents 1. Revels 1. Ceremonies 1. Armoury 1. Wardrobe 1. Ordinance 1.	
Gowns {	Masters of the Requests Chamberlains of the Exchequer	four. two.
Cloaks {	Gentlemen of the Privy-Chamber.	
Long Mantles with Hats, and Feathers {	Knights of the Bath	68.
	The Knight Marshal, *A rich Coat*.	
Cloaks {	Treasurer of }{ Master of the the Chamber }{ Jewel-House.	
	Barons Younger Sons.	
	Viscounts Younger Sons.	
Robes, and *Caps* {	Barons of the Exchequer	3.
Robes, Caps { and *Collars* {	Justices of both Benches, viz. King's Bench, and Common-Pleas	6.
Robes, Caps, { and *Collars* {	Lord chief Baron }{ Lord chief Justice of the of the Exchequer, }{ Common-Pleas.	
Gown {	Master of }{ Lord Chief Justice { *Robe, Cap* and the Rolls }{ of the King's Bench { *Collar*.	
Cloaks {	Knights of the Privy-Council.	
	Barons eldest Sons.	
	Earls Younger Sons.	
	Viscounts eldest Sons.	
	Kettle-Drums.	

Rich

Rich Coats { The King's Trumpets.

The Serjeant Trumpeter, with his Mace.

In their Coats { Two Purfivants at Arms.
of Arms

Cloaks { Barons   51.

Marquesses Younger Sons.

Earls eldest Sons.

In their Coats { Two Purfivants at Arms.
of Arms,

Vifcounts   7.

Dukes Younger Sons.

Marquesses eldest Sons.

In their Coats with { Two Heraulds.
Collars of SS.

Cloak { Earls   32.

Lord Chamberlain of the King's Houshold, *viz.* the
Earl of Manchester, *with his White Staff.*

Dukes eldest Sons.

In their Coats with { Two Heraulds

Marquess   of their Heralds
of Dorchester.   of Worcester.

In their Coats with { Two Heraulds.
Collars of SS.

Rich embroi- { The Duke of Buckingham.
dred Cloak

In their Coats with { Norroy, King } { Clarencieux, King
Collars of SS. { of Arms.   } { of Arms.

The Lord Treasurer } { The Lord Chancellor
with his white Staff } { *with the Purse.*

The Lord High Steward
(*viz.* the Duke of Ormond)
with his White Staff.

Broad-brim'd { A perfon reprefenting } { A perfon reprefenting
Caps, and Ro- { the Duke of Aquitain } { the Duke of Normandy
bes of Ermine {

The

The Lord Mayor of London, carrying the City Scepter, on the left hand, bareheaded.	Garter, principal King of Arms, bare-headed, in *His Coat, and Collar of SS.*	The Gentleman Usher with the black Rod, on the right Hand, bare-Headed in truh Cloak.

The Duke of York.

Serjeants at Arms with their Maces, 8 on a side from the Sword forwards in rich Cloaks.	The Earl of Northumberland, Lord Constable of England, *pro tempore,* on the left hand.	The Sword born by the Earl of Suffolk, Earl Marshal *pro tempore.*	The Earl of Lindsey, L O R D great Chamberlain on the right hand.

The Duke of Albemarle,
Master of the Horse, leading a spare-Horse.
Sir George Carteret, Vice-Chamberlain.

The Earl of Cleveland, Captain of Pensioners	The Earl of Norwich, Captain of the Guard.

The Lieutenant of the Pensioners.
The King's Horse-Guard.
The Lord General's Horse-Guard.

This is a true relation of the Order, in which His Majesty, and the Train, that attended Him, passed through the CITY. It could not, till now, be exactly described, by reason of some alteration from the first Design, not agreed on, till that very Morning.

F I N I S.